www.booksbyboxer.com

No part of this publication may be reproduced or transmitted in any form or by any means, electronic or mechanical, including photocopying, recording or any information storage and retrieval system, or for the source of ideas without written permission from the publisher.

Bee Three Publishing is an imprint of Books By Boxer
Published by
Books By Boxer, Leeds, LS13 4BS UK
Books by Boxer (EU), Dublin, D02 P593, IRELAND
Boxer Gifts LLC, 955 Sawtooth Oak Cir, VA 22802, USA
© Books By Boxer 2024
All Rights Reserved
MADE IN CHINA
ISBN: 9781915410313

This book is produced from responsibly sourced paper to ensure forest management

SAVE Water DRINK wine

WINE NAME .... **PRICE** ....

WINERY .... **VINTAGE** ....

ORIGIN .... **LOCATION DRUNK** ....

COLOR METER (CIRCLE BEST MATCH)

TASTE:
WOODY | TANNIC | TART | SWEET | SPICY | HERBAL | CITRUS | BERRY | OTHER ....

AROMA:
WOODY | TANNIC | TART | SWEET | SPICY | HERBAL | CITRUS | BERRY | OTHER ....

NOTES:
....
....
....

AFTERTASTE: ....

SMOOTH METER:

SMOOTH   HARSH

RATING: ☆ ☆ ☆ ☆ ☆ ☆ ☆ ☆ ☆ ☆

WINE NAME .... | **PRICE** ....

WINERY .... | **VINTAGE** ....

ORIGIN .... | **LOCATION DRUNK** ....

COLOR METER (CIRCLE BEST MATCH)

TASTE:
WOODY | TANNIC | TART | SWEET | SPICY | HERBAL | CITRUS | BERRY |
OTHER ....

AROMA:
WOODY | TANNIC | TART | SWEET | SPICY | HERBAL | CITRUS | BERRY |
OTHER ....

NOTES:
....
....
....

AFTERTASTE: .... | **SMOOTH METER:**
.... | SMOOTH ─────────────── HARSH

RATING: ☆ ☆ ☆ ☆ ☆ ☆ ☆ ☆ ☆ ☆

WINE NAME	**PRICE**
WINERY	**VINTAGE**
ORIGIN	**LOCATION DRUNK**

COLOR METER (CIRCLE BEST MATCH)

TASTE:

WOODY | TANNIC | TART | SWEET | SPICY | HERBAL | CITRUS | BERRY | OTHER

AROMA:

WOODY | TANNIC | TART | SWEET | SPICY | HERBAL | CITRUS | BERRY | OTHER

NOTES:

AFTERTASTE:

SMOOTH METER:

SMOOTH   HARSH

RATING: ☆ ☆ ☆ ☆ ☆ ☆ ☆ ☆ ☆ ☆

WINE NAME ....

WINERY ....

ORIGIN ....

PRICE ....

VINTAGE ....

LOCATION DRUNK ....

COLOR METER (CIRCLE BEST MATCH)

TASTE:
WOODY | TANNIC | TART | SWEET | SPICY | HERBAL | CITRUS | BERRY | OTHER ....

AROMA:
WOODY | TANNIC | TART | SWEET | SPICY | HERBAL | CITRUS | BERRY | OTHER ....

NOTES: ....
....
....

AFTERTASTE: ....

SMOOTH METER:

SMOOTH   HARSH

RATING: ☆ ☆ ☆ ☆ ☆ ☆ ☆ ☆ ☆ ☆

WINE NAME .... | **PRICE** ....
WINERY .... | **VINTAGE** ....
ORIGIN .... | **LOCATION DRUNK** ....

COLOR METER (CIRCLE BEST MATCH)

TASTE:
WOODY | TANNIC | TART | SWEET | SPICY | HERBAL | CITRUS | BERRY | OTHER

AROMA:
WOODY | TANNIC | TART | SWEET | SPICY | HERBAL | CITRUS | BERRY | OTHER

NOTES:

AFTERTASTE: .... | **SMOOTH METER:**
SMOOTH   HARSH

RATING: ☆ ☆ ☆ ☆ ☆ ☆ ☆ ☆ ☆ ☆

Sip, Spin, Discover!

Take a sip of that fine wine, and let the magic begin! The flavor wheel is like a map of taste, helping you navigate the intricate landscape of wine.

Just like spinning a wheel of fortune, except your prize is a symphony of flavors. Is it fruity, floral, or maybe a bit oaky?

Are you catching hints of berries, a touch of vanilla, or perhaps a subtle whisper of leather? It's like decoding a secret message from the grape gods!

Channel your inner wine detective. Explore the outer reaches of the wheel - is it more on the spicy side, or does it lean towards the earthy mysteries of the vineyard?

Now, armed with your newfound flavor knowledge, share the experience with fellow wine enthusiasts. Impress them with your ability to unravel the intricate tapestry of flavors, and let the wine flavor wheel be your conversation starter!

We've broken down the most common flavors found within wine to help you next time you want to look like a connoisseur and highlight a floral yet fruity note to your friends.

Primary flavors commonly come from the grape while the secondary flavors come from the wine making process imbued by the winemaker.

Sip & Learn:

Uncorking the Secrets
Behind Your Favorite Wines!

1. Wine was commonly drunk in favor over water in centuries past. At that time clean drinking water wasn't as readily available as it is today.

2. The world's oldest bottle of wine is on display in Speyer, a town in Germany close to where the bottle was located. The bottle dates to just before A.D. 325, and was unearthed from a Roman tomb.

3. King Tutankhamun was said to favor red wine, so much so he was buried with 26 pitchers of the stuff!

make time for wine

WINE NAME ....

WINERY ....

ORIGIN ....

PRICE ....

VINTAGE ....

LOCATION DRUNK ....

COLOR METER (CIRCLE BEST MATCH)

TASTE:
WOODY | TANNIC | TART | SWEET | SPICY | HERBAL | CITRUS | BERRY | OTHER ....

AROMA:
WOODY | TANNIC | TART | SWEET | SPICY | HERBAL | CITRUS | BERRY | OTHER ....

NOTES:
....
....
....

AFTERTASTE:
....
....

SMOOTH METER:
SMOOTH ☐☐☐☐☐☐☐ HARSH

RATING: ☆ ☆ ☆ ☆ ☆ ☆ ☆ ☆ ☆ ☆

WINE NAME .... **PRICE** ....

WINERY .... **VINTAGE** ....

ORIGIN .... **LOCATION DRUNK** ....

COLOR METER (CIRCLE BEST MATCH)

TASTE:
WOODY | TANNIC | TART | SWEET | SPICY | HERBAL | CITRUS | BERRY | OTHER ....

AROMA:
WOODY | TANNIC | TART | SWEET | SPICY | HERBAL | CITRUS | BERRY | OTHER ....

NOTES: ....
....
....

AFTERTASTE: ....

SMOOTH METER:

SMOOTH — HARSH

RATING: ☆ ☆ ☆ ☆ ☆ ☆ ☆ ☆ ☆ ☆

WINE NAME

WINERY

ORIGIN

PRICE

VINTAGE

LOCATION DRUNK

COLOR METER (CIRCLE BEST MATCH)

TASTE:
WOODY | TANNIC | TART | SWEET | SPICY | HERBAL | CITRUS | BERRY | OTHER

AROMA:
WOODY | TANNIC | TART | SWEET | SPICY | HERBAL | CITRUS | BERRY | OTHER

NOTES:

AFTERTASTE:

SMOOTH METER:

SMOOTH — HARSH

RATING:

WINE NAME ....

WINERY ....

ORIGIN ....

PRICE ....

VINTAGE ....

LOCATION DRUNK ....

COLOR METER (CIRCLE BEST MATCH)

TASTE:
WOODY | TANNIC | TART | SWEET | SPICY | HERBAL | CITRUS | BERRY |
OTHER ....

AROMA:
WOODY | TANNIC | TART | SWEET | SPICY | HERBAL | CITRUS | BERRY |
OTHER ....

NOTES: ....

....

....

AFTERTASTE: ....

....

SMOOTH METER:

| | | | | | | | |
SMOOTH HARSH

RATING: ☆ ☆ ☆ ☆ ☆ ☆ ☆ ☆ ☆ ☆

Hot or Cold?

Serving wine at the correct temperature enhances its notes and aromas, optimizing the drinking experience.

Full-bodied red wines, like Shiraz and Malbec, should be served at 65°F (18.5°C), while lighter reds, such as Pinot Noir and Zinfandel, are best at 60°F (15.5°C). Rosé is ideal at around 54°F (12°C) to highlight its subtle notes.

Full-bodied white wines, like Chardonnay and Viognier, should be served at 52°F (11°C), whereas lighter whites, such as Sauvignon Blanc and Pinot Grigio, are best at 46°F (7.5°C).

Sparkling wines are typically best served chilled straight from the refrigerator.

Looks Like It's Time For Wine

Oh, look a new glass of wine! Before you take that first sip here's what the appearance of the wine in your glass might tell you.

• If your wine is deeper in color whether red or white, this often suggests riper grapes have been used during production.

• Thick legs (how the wine trickles down the glass) usually indicate a sugary, high alcohol content wine.

If your wine is bubbly ...but it's non-sparkling, this usually suggests the wine is from a cooler climate.

White wine with a deep color is often older or indicates it was oak aged.

Various wine glasses

CHARDONNAY   HOCK   FLUTE

ROSÉ   BURGUNDY   CABERNET SAUVIGNON

STANDARD RED

STANDARD WHITE

STANDARD SWEET

MADEIRA

VINTAGE

TULIP

Wine and Cheese

WINE NAME .... **PRICE** ....

WINERY .... **VINTAGE** ....

ORIGIN .... **LOCATION DRUNK** ....

COLOR METER (CIRCLE BEST MATCH)

TASTE:

WOODY | TANNIC | TART | SWEET | SPICY | HERBAL | CITRUS | BERRY | OTHER ....

AROMA:

WOODY | TANNIC | TART | SWEET | SPICY | HERBAL | CITRUS | BERRY | OTHER ....

NOTES:

....

....

....

AFTERTASTE: ....

SMOOTH METER:

SMOOTH   HARSH

RATING: ☆ ☆ ☆ ☆ ☆ ☆ ☆ ☆ ☆ ☆

WINE NAME .... | **PRICE** ....

WINERY .... | **VINTAGE** ....

ORIGIN .... | **LOCATION DRUNK** ....

COLOR METER (CIRCLE BEST MATCH)

TASTE:
WOODY | TANNIC | TART | SWEET | SPICY | HERBAL | CITRUS | BERRY | OTHER ....

AROMA:
WOODY | TANNIC | TART | SWEET | SPICY | HERBAL | CITRUS | BERRY | OTHER ....

NOTES: ....

AFTERTASTE: .... | **SMOOTH METER:**
SMOOTH   HARSH

RATING: ☆ ☆ ☆ ☆ ☆ ☆ ☆ ☆ ☆ ☆

WINE NAME .... | **PRICE** ....

WINERY .... | **VINTAGE** ....

ORIGIN .... | **LOCATION DRUNK** ....

COLOR METER (CIRCLE BEST MATCH)

TASTE:
WOODY | TANNIC | TART | SWEET | SPICY | HERBAL | CITRUS | BERRY |
OTHER ....

AROMA:
WOODY | TANNIC | TART | SWEET | SPICY | HERBAL | CITRUS | BERRY |
OTHER ....

NOTES:
....
....
....

AFTERTASTE: .... | **SMOOTH METER:**
.... | SMOOTH   HARSH

RATING: ☆ ☆ ☆ ☆ ☆ ☆ ☆ ☆ ☆

WINE NAME .... **PRICE** ....

WINERY .... **VINTAGE** ....

ORIGIN .... **LOCATION DRUNK** ....

COLOR METER (CIRCLE BEST MATCH)

TASTE:
WOODY | TANNIC | TART | SWEET | SPICY | HERBAL | CITRUS | BERRY | OTHER

AROMA:
WOODY | TANNIC | TART | SWEET | SPICY | HERBAL | CITRUS | BERRY | OTHER

NOTES:

AFTERTASTE: .... **SMOOTH METER:**

SMOOTH   HARSH

RATING: ☆ ☆ ☆ ☆ ☆ ☆ ☆ ☆ ☆ ☆

WINE NAME .... | **PRICE** ....

WINERY .... | **VINTAGE** ....

ORIGIN .... | **LOCATION DRUNK** ....

COLOR METER (CIRCLE BEST MATCH)

TASTE:

WOODY | TANNIC | TART | SWEET | SPICY | HERBAL | CITRUS | BERRY | OTHER ....

AROMA:

WOODY | TANNIC | TART | SWEET | SPICY | HERBAL | CITRUS | BERRY | OTHER ....

NOTES:

....
....
....

AFTERTASTE: .... | **SMOOTH METER:**

SMOOTH ─────────────── HARSH

RATING: ☆ ☆ ☆ ☆ ☆ ☆ ☆ ☆ ☆ ☆

All Summer Long Sangria

What you'll need:

- 1 bottle of medium bodied red Spanish wine
- 120ml | ½ cup orange juice
- 60ml | ¼ cup brandy
- Juice of 1 lemon
- Orange wedge for garnish
- Selection of fruit chopped
  2 oranges
  1 apple
  1 pear
- 100g |¾ cup chopped cherries
- 100g |¾ cup chopped strawberries

Method:

Step 1: Add ice to your pitcher and pour in the red wine, orange juice, brandy, and lemon juice.

Step 2: Add your chopped fruit of choice and stir to combine.

Step 3: Squeeze your orange wedge into the glass and gently drop in to use as garnish, along with a few cubes of ice.

Step 4: Stir before serving.

Top tip:
Leave your Sangria in the fridge for 3 to 4 hours prior to serving to allow the flavors to combine for a more strong and authentic taste. Just stir before serving.

Sip & Learn:

Uncorking the Secrets
Behind Your Favorite Wines!

1. May 25th is often celebrated as
National Wine Day!

2. To ensure that the wine served to guests wasn't poisoned, ancient Greek hosts would take the first sip of the wine. This act has been cited to be why we have the phrase "drinking to one's health".

3. The Vatican City has the highest per capita wine consumption rate in the world.

CORKS are for QUITTERS

WINE NAME .... **PRICE** ....

WINERY .... **VINTAGE** ....

ORIGIN .... **LOCATION DRUNK** ....

COLOR METER (CIRCLE BEST MATCH)

TASTE:

WOODY | TANNIC | TART | SWEET | SPICY | HERBAL | CITRUS | BERRY |
OTHER ....

AROMA:

WOODY | TANNIC | TART | SWEET | SPICY | HERBAL | CITRUS | BERRY |
OTHER ....

NOTES:

....
....
....
....

AFTERTASTE: .... | **SMOOTH METER:**

SMOOTH   HARSH

RATING: ☆ ☆ ☆ ☆ ☆ ☆ ☆ ☆ ☆ ☆

WINE NAME ....

WINERY ....

ORIGIN ....

PRICE ....

VINTAGE ....

LOCATION DRUNK ....

COLOR METER (CIRCLE BEST MATCH)

TASTE:
WOODY | TANNIC | TART | SWEET | SPICY | HERBAL | CITRUS | BERRY | OTHER ....

AROMA:
WOODY | TANNIC | TART | SWEET | SPICY | HERBAL | CITRUS | BERRY | OTHER ....

NOTES: ....
....
....

AFTERTASTE: ....

SMOOTH METER:

SMOOTH   HARSH

RATING: ☆ ☆ ☆ ☆ ☆ ☆ ☆ ☆ ☆ ☆

WINE NAME .... **PRICE** ....

WINERY .... **VINTAGE** ....

ORIGIN .... **LOCATION DRUNK** ....

COLOR METER (CIRCLE BEST MATCH)

TASTE:

WOODY | TANNIC | TART | SWEET | SPICY | HERBAL | CITRUS | BERRY | OTHER ....

AROMA:

WOODY | TANNIC | TART | SWEET | SPICY | HERBAL | CITRUS | BERRY | OTHER ....

NOTES:

....

....

....

AFTERTASTE: ....

SMOOTH METER:

SMOOTH .... HARSH

RATING: ☆ ☆ ☆ ☆ ☆ ☆ ☆ ☆ ☆ ☆

WINE NAME .... **PRICE** ....

WINERY .... **VINTAGE** ....

ORIGIN .... **LOCATION DRUNK** ....

COLOR METER (CIRCLE BEST MATCH)

TASTE:
WOODY | TANNIC | TART | SWEET | SPICY | HERBAL | CITRUS | BERRY | OTHER ....

AROMA:
WOODY | TANNIC | TART | SWEET | SPICY | HERBAL | CITRUS | BERRY | OTHER ....

NOTES: ....

....

....

AFTERTASTE: .... | **SMOOTH METER:**
| SMOOTH   HARSH

RATING: ☆ ☆ ☆ ☆ ☆ ☆ ☆ ☆ ☆ ☆

Serve Wine Like A Pro

- Use the appropriate glass for the type of wine you are serving (red, white, sparkling, etc.).

- Ensure the wine is at the correct serving temperature. Reds are typically served slightly cooler, while whites and sparkling wines are served chilled.

- Use a good quality corkscrew or wine opener. Remove the cork smoothly without breaking it.

- Hold the bottle by the lower half or the base, not the neck. This gives you better control and prevents your hand from warming the wine.

- Start pouring gently, allowing the wine to flow smoothly into the glass without splashing.

- For red wine, fill the glass about one-third full to allow space for swirling. For white wine, fill it about halfway. For sparkling wine, fill it about three-quarters full to prevent overflow of bubbles.

The more you practice, the more comfortable and professional you will become at pouring wine.

White Wines:

Always buying the same kind of wine but you want to branch out? Here's a list of a few wine types.

Pinto Grigio:
Light-bodied wine described as crisp and dry, with notes of peach and hints of pear.

Riesling:
A light bodied, very sweet wine usually with intense fruity flavors.

Chardonnay:
A medium to full bodied white wine. Dry with fruity flavors, often described as buttery

Sauvignon Blanc:
A dry, light to medium bodied high-acidity wine with tropical citrus notes.

Chenin Blanc:
Versatile wine that can be dry, sweet or sparkling. With apple, pear, and floral notes.

Red Wines:

Merlot:

Medium to full-bodied with softer tannins, with notes of plum, black cherry, raspberry, and chocolate.

Cabernet Sauvignon:

Full-bodied with high tannins and acidity with notes of blackberry, cedar, tobacco, and dark chocolate.

Pinot Noir:

Light to medium-bodied with high acidity, with cherry, raspberry, strawberry flavors, and earthy notes.

Zinfandel:

Medium to full-bodied with moderate tannins, filled with spice notes, with raspberry, and black pepper flavors.

Shiraz:

Full-bodied with medium to high tannins, flavors ranging from blackberry and blueberry, to black pepper and smoked meat notes

Sip me baby one more time

WINE NAME		**PRICE**
WINERY		**VINTAGE**
ORIGIN		**LOCATION DRUNK**

COLOR METER (CIRCLE BEST MATCH)

TASTE:

WOODY | TANNIC | TART | SWEET | SPICY | HERBAL | CITRUS | BERRY | OTHER

AROMA:

WOODY | TANNIC | TART | SWEET | SPICY | HERBAL | CITRUS | BERRY | OTHER

NOTES:

AFTERTASTE:

SMOOTH METER:

SMOOTH   HARSH

RATING: ☆ ☆ ☆ ☆ ☆ ☆ ☆ ☆ ☆ ☆

WINE NAME	**PRICE**
WINERY	**VINTAGE**
ORIGIN	**LOCATION DRUNK**

COLOR METER (CIRCLE BEST MATCH)

TASTE:
WOODY | TANNIC | TART | SWEET | SPICY | HERBAL | CITRUS | BERRY | OTHER

AROMA:
WOODY | TANNIC | TART | SWEET | SPICY | HERBAL | CITRUS | BERRY | OTHER

NOTES:

AFTERTASTE:

SMOOTH METER:
SMOOTH .... HARSH

RATING: ☆ ☆ ☆ ☆ ☆ ☆ ☆ ☆ ☆ ☆

WINE NAME	**PRICE** ....
WINERY	**VINTAGE** ....
ORIGIN	**LOCATION DRUNK** ....

COLOR METER (CIRCLE BEST MATCH)

TASTE:

WOODY | TANNIC | TART | SWEET | SPICY | HERBAL | CITRUS | BERRY | OTHER ....

AROMA:

WOODY | TANNIC | TART | SWEET | SPICY | HERBAL | CITRUS | BERRY | OTHER ....

NOTES: ....
....
....

AFTERTASTE: ....

SMOOTH METER:

SMOOTH ⟶ HARSH

RATING: ☆ ☆ ☆ ☆ ☆ ☆ ☆ ☆ ☆ ☆

WINE NAME	**PRICE**
WINERY	**VINTAGE**
ORIGIN	**LOCATION DRUNK**

COLOR METER (CIRCLE BEST MATCH)

TASTE:

WOODY | TANNIC | TART | SWEET | SPICY | HERBAL | CITRUS | BERRY | OTHER

AROMA:

WOODY | TANNIC | TART | SWEET | SPICY | HERBAL | CITRUS | BERRY | OTHER

NOTES:

AFTERTASTE:

SMOOTH METER:

SMOOTH   HARSH

RATING: ☆ ☆ ☆ ☆ ☆ ☆ ☆ ☆ ☆ ☆

Smell Like A Sommelier

First stop to becoming a wine expert is learning the lingo. When discussing fragrances, aroma is the term used to describe fragrance of young wine, but mellow is the term used for old wine.

The next step is only filling your glass by a third, this allows space for aromas to collect after you have swirled your wine in the glass.

The last step is knowing some key elements to look for, here are some examples:

- Fruit – can you identify what kind of fruit such as tropical or red berries?

- Spices or nutty notes.

- Flowers.

- Rich notes such as tobacco or coffee.

- Or any off smells such as a vinegar.

Yes Way, Frosé

What you'll need:

- 1 bottle of dry Rosé wine
- 300g | 2 cups halved strawberries
- 50g | ¼ cup granulated sugar
- Juice of 1 lemon

Method:

Step 1: Carefully pour 1 bottle of your Rosé of choice into a deep freezer safe tin or container and leave overnight.

Step 2: 30 minutes before you're ready to serve, mix the strawberries together with the sugar until coated.

Step 3: Once your strawberries have begun to release their juices after 30 minutes, combine with the lemon juice and your frozen rosé wine into a blender and blitz.

Step 4: Divide your mixture between 4 glasses and enjoy!

Sip & Learn:

Uncorking the Secrets
Behind Your Favorite Wines!

1. California is the 4th largest producer of wine in the world and has over 4500 wineries (and produces 80% of all wine made in the U.S!)

2. Most wines are not intended to be aged. Many wines produced now are best enjoyed within 5 years; only an estimated 10% of wines produced today benefit from the stereotypical aging.

3. Most wines aren't naturally vegan. Animal by products are often used as fining agents to stabilize the wine, and whilst mainly processed out, some traces may get left in the wine.

Sip BACK And Relax

WINE NAME	**PRICE**
WINERY	**VINTAGE**
ORIGIN	**LOCATION DRUNK**

COLOR METER (CIRCLE BEST MATCH)

TASTE:
WOODY | TANNIC | TART | SWEET | SPICY | HERBAL | CITRUS | BERRY | OTHER

AROMA:
WOODY | TANNIC | TART | SWEET | SPICY | HERBAL | CITRUS | BERRY | OTHER

NOTES:

AFTERTASTE:

SMOOTH METER:
SMOOTH — HARSH

RATING: ☆ ☆ ☆ ☆ ☆ ☆ ☆ ☆ ☆ ☆

WINE NAME .... | **PRICE** ....

WINERY .... | **VINTAGE** ....

ORIGIN .... | **LOCATION DRUNK** ....

COLOR METER (CIRCLE BEST MATCH)

TASTE:
WOODY | TANNIC | TART | SWEET | SPICY | HERBAL | CITRUS | BERRY |
OTHER ....

AROMA:
WOODY | TANNIC | TART | SWEET | SPICY | HERBAL | CITRUS | BERRY |
OTHER ....

NOTES:
....
....
....

AFTERTASTE: ....

SMOOTH METER:

SMOOTH — HARSH

RATING: ☆ ☆ ☆ ☆ ☆ ☆ ☆ ☆ ☆ ☆

WINE NAME .... | **PRICE** ....

WINERY .... | **VINTAGE** ....

ORIGIN .... | **LOCATION DRUNK** ....

COLOR METER (CIRCLE BEST MATCH)

TASTE:
WOODY | TANNIC | TART | SWEET | SPICY | HERBAL | CITRUS | BERRY | OTHER ....

AROMA:
WOODY | TANNIC | TART | SWEET | SPICY | HERBAL | CITRUS | BERRY | OTHER ....

NOTES:

....

....

AFTERTASTE: ....

SMOOTH METER:

SMOOTH .... HARSH

RATING: ☆ ☆ ☆ ☆ ☆ ☆ ☆ ☆ ☆ ☆

WINE NAME .... **PRICE** ....

WINERY .... **VINTAGE** ....

ORIGIN .... **LOCATION DRUNK** ....

COLOR METER (CIRCLE BEST MATCH)

TASTE:
WOODY | TANNIC | TART | SWEET | SPICY | HERBAL | CITRUS | BERRY |
OTHER ....

AROMA:
WOODY | TANNIC | TART | SWEET | SPICY | HERBAL | CITRUS | BERRY |
OTHER ....

NOTES:
....
....
....

AFTERTASTE: .... **SMOOTH METER:**

SMOOTH ———————————— HARSH

RATING: ☆ ☆ ☆ ☆ ☆ ☆ ☆ ☆ ☆ ☆

Stop & Smell The Rosé

Use a white wine glass or a glass specifically designed for rosé. A glass with a slightly tapered top helps concentrate the aromas.

Hold the glass against a white background to examine the color. Rosé wines can range from pale pink to vibrant salmon. The color can give you clues about the wine's style and potential flavors.

Gently swirl the wine in the glass. This helps release the aromas, making it easier to smell.

Rosé wines are typically light to medium-bodied. They often have a crisp acidity, which makes them refreshing. Notice how the acidity balances with the fruit flavors.

Rosé wine is best served chilled, usually between 45-55ºF (7-13ºC). This temperature range helps to highlight its refreshing qualities and aromas.

Vino Vocab

Embarking on a journey through the world of wine lingo is like stumbling into a linguistic vineyard, where each term is a grape waiting to be plucked.

Acidity:

The part of the wine that makes your mouth water when you drink it.

Body:

The structure of the wine and its viscosity and mouthfeel.

Length:

How long you can taste the wine after swallowing or spitting it out.

Big:

A wine that is full of everything: flavor, alcohol, tannin and oak.

Closed:

When the wine doesn't provide many aromas when smelling it.

Crisp:
High acid content.

Delicate:
The opposite of big, meaning the flavors are subtle and light.

Length:
A medium to full bodied white wine. Dry with fruity flavors, often described as buttery.

Legs:
The wine residue that sticks to the side of the glass when swirling. This is usually an indicator of sugar content!

Soft:
Low acidity.

Oaky:
Usually a sign of the aging process. Oaky wines may have notes of spice, vanilla, and smoke.

Tannins:
A quality of the wine that comes from the skins. A high tannin wine can be dry on the tongue and rich or chalky on the palette.

WINE NAME

WINERY

ORIGIN

PRICE

VINTAGE

LOCATION DRUNK

COLOR METER (CIRCLE BEST MATCH)

TASTE:

WOODY | TANNIC | TART | SWEET | SPICY | HERBAL | CITRUS | BERRY | OTHER

AROMA:

WOODY | TANNIC | TART | SWEET | SPICY | HERBAL | CITRUS | BERRY | OTHER

NOTES:

AFTERTASTE:

SMOOTH METER:

SMOOTH   HARSH

RATING:

WINE NAME .... | **PRICE** ....

WINERY .... | **VINTAGE** ....

ORIGIN .... | **LOCATION DRUNK** ....

COLOR METER (CIRCLE BEST MATCH)

TASTE:
WOODY | TANNIC | TART | SWEET | SPICY | HERBAL | CITRUS | BERRY | OTHER ....

AROMA:
WOODY | TANNIC | TART | SWEET | SPICY | HERBAL | CITRUS | BERRY | OTHER ....

NOTES: ....
....
....

AFTERTASTE: .... | **SMOOTH METER:**
.... | SMOOTH   HARSH

RATING: ☆ ☆ ☆ ☆ ☆ ☆ ☆ ☆ ☆ ☆

WINE NAME .... | **PRICE** ....

WINERY .... | **VINTAGE** ....

ORIGIN .... | **LOCATION DRUNK** ....

COLOR METER (CIRCLE BEST MATCH)

TASTE:
WOODY | TANNIC | TART | SWEET | SPICY | HERBAL | CITRUS | BERRY | OTHER ....

AROMA:
WOODY | TANNIC | TART | SWEET | SPICY | HERBAL | CITRUS | BERRY | OTHER ....

NOTES:
....
....
....

AFTERTASTE: .... | **SMOOTH METER:**
SMOOTH ─────────── HARSH

RATING: ☆ ☆ ☆ ☆ ☆ ☆ ☆ ☆ ☆ ☆

Taste Test

On your wine-tasting journey, consider these questions to unravel the intricate layers of flavors, textures, and sensations that await:

Body:
Is the wine thick and weighty on your palate, or does it glide down like a refreshing sip of water? Full-bodied wines often hail from warmer climates, offering a rich and luxurious experience that lingers on the tongue.

Sweetness:
Wines with a noticeable sweetness may derive from a late harvest, capturing the essence of sun-kissed grapes.

Bitterness:
Does a hint of bitterness make its presence known? Embrace the complexity; bitterness can add depth and character to the overall profile.

Acidity:
Wines with high acidity often originate from cooler climates, showcasing a vibrant and lively character.

Tannins:
Strong tannins might leave a dry sensation, offering insight into the grape variety or the region where the wine was crafted.

Warmth:
Warmth is often a telltale sign of a higher alcohol level, adding a touch of intensity to your tasting adventure.

Finish:
A lingering finish, like the final notes of a symphony, often signals a wine crafted from full-flavored grapes, hinting at a higher quality and a memorable experience.

Mulled Wine & Mince Pies

What you'll need:

- 1 bottle (750 ml) red wine
- ¼ cup brandy (optional)
- ¼ cup honey or sugar (adjust to taste)
- 1 orange, sliced
- 1 lemon, sliced
- 8 whole cloves
- 2 cinnamon sticks
- 2 star anise

Optional garnish: orange or lemon slices, cinnamon sticks

Method:

Step 1: In a large saucepan or pot, pour the red wine and add the sugar. Stir until the sugar dissolves.

Step 2: Add the sliced orange and lemon, whole cloves, cinnamon sticks, and star anise to the pot. Stir to combine.

Step 3: Place the saucepan over medium heat. Heat the mulled wine mixture gently, but do not boil. Let it simmer for about 15-20 minutes to allow the flavors to meld together.

Step 4: As the mulled wine simmers, the spices will infuse the wine with their flavors, creating a warm and aromatic beverage.

Step 5 (optional): If desired, add the brandy or orange liqueur to the mulled wine for extra warmth and flavor. Stir to combine.

Once heated through and infused with flavor, remove the mulled wine from the heat. Ladle it into mugs or heatproof glasses, making sure to include some of the sliced fruit and spices in each serving.

Optional: Garnish each mug with a slice of orange or lemon and a cinnamon stick for an extra festive touch.

you had me at merlot

WINE NAME .... **PRICE** ....

WINERY .... **VINTAGE** ....

ORIGIN .... **LOCATION DRUNK** ....

COLOR METER (CIRCLE BEST MATCH)

TASTE:

WOODY | TANNIC | TART | SWEET | SPICY | HERBAL | CITRUS | BERRY | OTHER ....

AROMA:

WOODY | TANNIC | TART | SWEET | SPICY | HERBAL | CITRUS | BERRY | OTHER ....

NOTES: ....

....

....

....

AFTERTASTE: .... **SMOOTH METER:**

.... SMOOTH   HARSH

RATING: ☆ ☆ ☆ ☆ ☆ ☆ ☆ ☆ ☆ ☆

WINE NAME .... **PRICE** ....

WINERY .... **VINTAGE** ....

ORIGIN .... **LOCATION DRUNK** ....

COLOR METER (CIRCLE BEST MATCH)

TASTE:
WOODY | TANNIC | TART | SWEET | SPICY | HERBAL | CITRUS | BERRY |
OTHER ....

AROMA:
WOODY | TANNIC | TART | SWEET | SPICY | HERBAL | CITRUS | BERRY |
OTHER ....

NOTES: ....

....

....

AFTERTASTE: ....

SMOOTH METER:

SMOOTH   HARSH

RATING: ☆ ☆ ☆ ☆ ☆ ☆ ☆ ☆ ☆ ☆

WINE NAME .... | **PRICE** ....

WINERY .... | **VINTAGE** ....

ORIGIN .... | **LOCATION DRUNK** ....

COLOR METER (CIRCLE BEST MATCH)

TASTE:
WOODY | TANNIC | TART | SWEET | SPICY | HERBAL | CITRUS | BERRY | OTHER ....

AROMA:
WOODY | TANNIC | TART | SWEET | SPICY | HERBAL | CITRUS | BERRY | OTHER ....

NOTES:
....
....
....

AFTERTASTE: ....

SMOOTH METER:
SMOOTH ─────────── HARSH

RATING: ☆ ☆ ☆ ☆ ☆ ☆ ☆ ☆ ☆ ☆

WINE NAME ....

WINERY ....

ORIGIN ....

PRICE ....

VINTAGE ....

LOCATION DRUNK ....

COLOR METER (CIRCLE BEST MATCH)

TASTE:
WOODY | TANNIC | TART | SWEET | SPICY | HERBAL | CITRUS | BERRY | OTHER ....

AROMA:
WOODY | TANNIC | TART | SWEET | SPICY | HERBAL | CITRUS | BERRY | OTHER ....

NOTES:
....
....
....

AFTERTASTE:
....
....

SMOOTH METER:

SMOOTH — HARSH

RATING: ☆ ☆ ☆ ☆ ☆ ☆ ☆ ☆ ☆ ☆

What's in a Smell?

When you open a bottle of wine, the aroma it releases can reveal a lot about its origin and production. Pay attention to the following smells during your next wine experience.

Is there a toasty scent in your white wine, or do you detect tobacco or developed spices in your red? These are often indications that the wine is older or has been aged in oak, which typically adds nutty and vanilla notes.

You can also identify the grape variety or region by distinct aromas. For instance, an earthy note often indicates that the wine is from Bordeaux, while Sauvignon Blanc typically has a green pepper tang, and Cabernet Sauvignon boasts red berry aromas, such as blackcurrants.

Finally, consider the climate in which the wine was produced. Wines made in warm climates often have rich and jammy fruit flavors.

Which Wine When?

Bold Red
Cabernet Sauvignon

Syrah

Malbec

Light White
Albarino

Sauvignon Blanc

Pinot Gris

Rich White
Chardonnay

Viognier

Marsanne

Rose
Provence Rose

White Zinfandel

Bandol Rose

Matching your wine to your meal can seem daunting, but following these simple breakdowns should help you perfect your pairings!

Sparkling
Champagne

Prosecco

Cava

Sweet
Mascato

Riesling
Late Harvest Whites

Amber
Vinho de Talha

Friulano

Kisi

Fortified
Port

Sherry

Vin Santo

Wine is Always a Good Idea

WINE NAME	**PRICE**
WINERY	**VINTAGE**
ORIGIN	**LOCATION DRUNK**

COLOR METER (CIRCLE BEST MATCH)

TASTE:

WOODY | TANNIC | TART | SWEET | SPICY | HERBAL | CITRUS | BERRY | OTHER

AROMA:

WOODY | TANNIC | TART | SWEET | SPICY | HERBAL | CITRUS | BERRY | OTHER

NOTES:

AFTERTASTE:

SMOOTH METER:

SMOOTH   HARSH

RATING: ☆ ☆ ☆ ☆ ☆ ☆ ☆ ☆ ☆ ☆

WINE NAME	**PRICE**
WINERY	**VINTAGE**
ORIGIN	**LOCATION DRUNK**

COLOR METER (CIRCLE BEST MATCH)

TASTE:
WOODY | TANNIC | TART | SWEET | SPICY | HERBAL | CITRUS | BERRY | OTHER

AROMA:
WOODY | TANNIC | TART | SWEET | SPICY | HERBAL | CITRUS | BERRY | OTHER

NOTES:

AFTERTASTE:

SMOOTH METER:

SMOOTH · · · · · · · · HARSH

RATING: ☆ ☆ ☆ ☆ ☆ ☆ ☆ ☆ ☆ ☆

WINE NAME .... | **PRICE** ....

WINERY .... | **VINTAGE** ....

ORIGIN .... | **LOCATION DRUNK** ....

COLOR METER (CIRCLE BEST MATCH)

TASTE:
WOODY | TANNIC | TART | SWEET | SPICY | HERBAL | CITRUS | BERRY |
OTHER ....

AROMA:
WOODY | TANNIC | TART | SWEET | SPICY | HERBAL | CITRUS | BERRY |
OTHER ....

NOTES: ....
....
....

AFTERTASTE: .... | **SMOOTH METER:**
                                  SMOOTH   HARSH

RATING: ☆ ☆ ☆ ☆ ☆ ☆ ☆ ☆ ☆ ☆

WINE NAME ....   **PRICE** ....

WINERY ....   **VINTAGE** ....

ORIGIN ....   **LOCATION DRUNK** ....

COLOR METER (CIRCLE BEST MATCH)

TASTE:

WOODY | TANNIC | TART | SWEET | SPICY | HERBAL | CITRUS | BERRY | OTHER ....

AROMA:

WOODY | TANNIC | TART | SWEET | SPICY | HERBAL | CITRUS | BERRY | OTHER ....

NOTES:
....
....
....
....

AFTERTASTE:
....
....

SMOOTH METER:

SMOOTH   HARSH

RATING: ☆ ☆ ☆ ☆ ☆ ☆ ☆ ☆ ☆ ☆

WINE NAME .... | **PRICE** ....

WINERY .... | **VINTAGE** ....

ORIGIN .... | **LOCATION DRUNK** ....

COLOR METER (CIRCLE BEST MATCH)

TASTE:

WOODY | TANNIC | TART | SWEET | SPICY | HERBAL | CITRUS | BERRY | OTHER ....

AROMA:

WOODY | TANNIC | TART | SWEET | SPICY | HERBAL | CITRUS | BERRY | OTHER ....

NOTES:

....

....

....

AFTERTASTE: | **SMOOTH METER:**

.... | SMOOTH .... HARSH

RATING: ☆ ☆ ☆ ☆ ☆ ☆ ☆ ☆ ☆ ☆

Sip & Learn:

Uncorking the Secrets
Behind Your Favorite Wines!

1. There are over 10,000 known grape varieties to exist across the globe. Not surprising, when you learn that grapes are the most planted fruit all over the world!

2. White wine doesn't need to come from white grapes. It's actually a process in the fermentation that makes the wine white, only the juices from the grapes are fermented and not the skins.

3. 'New World' wines are classified as wines from the Americas, Australasia, Africa and Asia, while 'Old World' wines are from Europe and the Middle East.

But First Mimosas

What you'll need:

- 1 ½ oz Aperol
- 3 oz chilled prosecco
- ½ oz fresh orange juice
- Orange slice or twist for garnish

Method:

Step 1: Make sure your Aperol, prosecco, and orange juice are well-chilled. You can place the prosecco in the refrigerator a few hours before serving.

Step 2: Take a champagne flute or a wine glass and chill it in the freezer for a few minutes.

Step 3: Measure and pour 1 ½ oz of Aperol into the chilled glass.

Step 4: Pour ½ oz of fresh orange juice into the glass. Adjust the amount based on your preference for sweetness.

Step 5: Gently pour 3 oz of chilled prosecco into the glass. Pour it slowly to maintain the effervescence.

Garnish the cocktail with an orange slice or a twist for a citrusy aroma. Traditionally, Mimosas are served without ice, but add some ice cubes if you'd prefer a chilled drink!

Serve and enjoy!

Wine a LITTLE Laugh A LOT

WINE NAME	PRICE
WINERY	VINTAGE
ORIGIN	LOCATION DRUNK

COLOR METER (CIRCLE BEST MATCH)

TASTE:
WOODY | TANNIC | TART | SWEET | SPICY | HERBAL | CITRUS | BERRY | OTHER

AROMA:
WOODY | TANNIC | TART | SWEET | SPICY | HERBAL | CITRUS | BERRY | OTHER

NOTES:

AFTERTASTE:

SMOOTH METER:
SMOOTH   HARSH

RATING: ☆ ☆ ☆ ☆ ☆ ☆ ☆ ☆ ☆ ☆

WINE NAME ....   **PRICE** ....

WINERY ....   **VINTAGE** ....

ORIGIN ....   **LOCATION DRUNK** ....

COLOR METER (CIRCLE BEST MATCH)

TASTE:

WOODY | TANNIC | TART | SWEET | SPICY | HERBAL | CITRUS | BERRY | OTHER ....

AROMA:

WOODY | TANNIC | TART | SWEET | SPICY | HERBAL | CITRUS | BERRY | OTHER ....

NOTES:

....

....

....

AFTERTASTE: ....   **SMOOTH METER:**

SMOOTH   HARSH

RATING: ☆ ☆ ☆ ☆ ☆ ☆ ☆ ☆ ☆ ☆

WINE NAME .... **PRICE** ....

WINERY .... **VINTAGE** ....

ORIGIN .... **LOCATION DRUNK** ....

COLOR METER (CIRCLE BEST MATCH)

TASTE:

WOODY | TANNIC | TART | SWEET | SPICY | HERBAL | CITRUS | BERRY | OTHER ....

AROMA:

WOODY | TANNIC | TART | SWEET | SPICY | HERBAL | CITRUS | BERRY | OTHER ....

NOTES:

....

....

....

AFTERTASTE:

....

SMOOTH METER:

SMOOTH ──────────── HARSH

RATING: ☆ ☆ ☆ ☆ ☆ ☆ ☆ ☆ ☆ ☆

WINE NAME	PRICE ....
WINERY	VINTAGE ....
ORIGIN	LOCATION DRUNK ....

COLOR METER (CIRCLE BEST MATCH)

TASTE:
WOODY | TANNIC | TART | SWEET | SPICY | HERBAL | CITRUS | BERRY | OTHER ....

AROMA:
WOODY | TANNIC | TART | SWEET | SPICY | HERBAL | CITRUS | BERRY | OTHER ....

NOTES:
....
....
....

AFTERTASTE:
....

SMOOTH METER:

SMOOTH   HARSH

RATING: ☆ ☆ ☆ ☆ ☆ ☆ ☆ ☆ ☆ ☆

WINE NAME .... **PRICE** ....

WINERY .... **VINTAGE** ....

ORIGIN .... **LOCATION DRUNK** ....

COLOR METER (CIRCLE BEST MATCH)

TASTE:

WOODY | TANNIC | TART | SWEET | SPICY | HERBAL | CITRUS | BERRY | OTHER ....

AROMA:

WOODY | TANNIC | TART | SWEET | SPICY | HERBAL | CITRUS | BERRY | OTHER ....

NOTES: ....

....

....

AFTERTASTE: .... **SMOOTH METER:**

SMOOTH   HARSH

RATING: ☆ ☆ ☆ ☆ ☆ ☆ ☆ ☆ ☆ ☆

Sip & Learn:

Uncorking the Secrets
Behind Your Favorite Wines!

1. The glass used to make Champagne bottles is usually thicker than the standard wine bottle, this helps protect against the pressure created by the carbonation.

2. In 2018 at an auction at Sotheby's, a 1945 vintage bottle of Romanée-Conti sold for a record breaking US $558,000.00. In the same auction, a second bottle of the same vintage was sold for US $ 496,000.00!

3. During the prohibition in the US, wine makers sold wine bricks. The bricks were sold as non-alcoholic with very clear instructions on how not to allow fermentation which would change the wine to be alcoholic; so clear they were very easy to follow in the opposite manner!

Spritz Up Your Life

What you'll need:
- 2 oz (60 ml) Limoncello liqueur
- 3 oz (90 ml) prosecco (chilled)
- 1 oz (30 ml) club soda (chilled)
- Ice cubes
- Lemon slices for garnish
- Fresh mint leaves for garnish

Method:

Step 1: Fill a glass (typically a wine glass or a large balloon glass) with ice cubes. This will keep your Limoncello Spritz nice and cold.

Step 2: Pour 2 ounces (60 ml) of Limoncello liqueur over the ice in the glass.

Step 3: Pour 3 ounces (90 ml) of Prosecco or any sparkling wine over the Limoncello in the glass.

Step 4: Top the drink with a splash of club soda or sparkling water. This adds a bit of effervescence and lightens the drink.

Step 5: Garnish the Limoncello Spritz with a slice of lemon for an extra burst of citrus flavor. You can also add a sprig of fresh mint for a touch of freshness if desired.

Step 6: Give the drink a gentle stir to combine all the ingredients.

Your Limoncello Spritz is ready to be enjoyed!

Drink WINE Feel FINE

WINE NAME .... | **PRICE** ....

WINERY .... | **VINTAGE** ....

ORIGIN .... | **LOCATION DRUNK** ....

COLOR METER (CIRCLE BEST MATCH)

TASTE:

WOODY | TANNIC | TART | SWEET | SPICY | HERBAL | CITRUS | BERRY | OTHER ....

AROMA:

WOODY | TANNIC | TART | SWEET | SPICY | HERBAL | CITRUS | BERRY | OTHER ....

NOTES:
....
....
....

AFTERTASTE: .... | **SMOOTH METER:**

SMOOTH — HARSH

RATING: ☆ ☆ ☆ ☆ ☆ ☆ ☆ ☆ ☆

WINE NAME .... | **PRICE** ....

WINERY .... | **VINTAGE** ....

ORIGIN .... | **LOCATION DRUNK** ....

COLOR METER (CIRCLE BEST MATCH)

TASTE:

WOODY | TANNIC | TART | SWEET | SPICY | HERBAL | CITRUS | BERRY | OTHER

AROMA:

WOODY | TANNIC | TART | SWEET | SPICY | HERBAL | CITRUS | BERRY | OTHER

NOTES:

AFTERTASTE: .... | **SMOOTH METER:**

SMOOTH   HARSH

RATING: ☆ ☆ ☆ ☆ ☆ ☆ ☆ ☆ ☆ ☆

WINE NAME ....   **PRICE** ....

WINERY ....   **VINTAGE** ....

ORIGIN ....   **LOCATION DRUNK** ....

COLOR METER (CIRCLE BEST MATCH)

TASTE:

WOODY | TANNIC | TART | SWEET | SPICY | HERBAL | CITRUS | BERRY | OTHER ....

AROMA:

WOODY | TANNIC | TART | SWEET | SPICY | HERBAL | CITRUS | BERRY | OTHER ....

NOTES: ....
....
....

AFTERTASTE: ....   **SMOOTH METER:**

SMOOTH   HARSH

RATING: ☆ ☆ ☆ ☆ ☆ ☆ ☆ ☆ ☆ ☆

WINE NAME .... **PRICE** ....

WINERY .... **VINTAGE** ....

ORIGIN .... **LOCATION DRUNK** ....

COLOR METER (CIRCLE BEST MATCH)

TASTE:
WOODY | TANNIC | TART | SWEET | SPICY | HERBAL | CITRUS | BERRY | OTHER ....

AROMA:
WOODY | TANNIC | TART | SWEET | SPICY | HERBAL | CITRUS | BERRY | OTHER ....

NOTES:
....
....
....

AFTERTASTE: ....

SMOOTH METER:

SMOOTH   HARSH

RATING: ☆ ☆ ☆ ☆ ☆ ☆ ☆ ☆ ☆ ☆

WINE NAME .... | **PRICE** ....

WINERY .... | **VINTAGE** ....

ORIGIN .... | **LOCATION DRUNK** ....

COLOR METER (CIRCLE BEST MATCH)

TASTE:

WOODY | TANNIC | TART | SWEET | SPICY | HERBAL | CITRUS | BERRY | OTHER ....

AROMA:

WOODY | TANNIC | TART | SWEET | SPICY | HERBAL | CITRUS | BERRY | OTHER ....

NOTES:
....
....
....

AFTERTASTE: .... | **SMOOTH METER:**
.... | SMOOTH ─────────── HARSH

RATING: ☆ ☆ ☆ ☆ ☆ ☆ ☆ ☆ ☆

How Wine is Made:

HARVEST YOUR GRAPES:
During the grape harvest, the most important thing to do is to pick the grapes at perfect ripeness.

PREPARE THE GRAPES:
The winemaker decides whether or not to remove the stems or to ferment grape bunches as whole clusters.

DESTEM THE GRAPES:
This is an important choice because leaving stems in the fermentation adds astringency, but also reduces sourness.

FERMENTATION:
Grape skins give the wine its color and flavor. So, during the fermentation, vinters punch down grapes or pump-over the must, so the skins stay submerged.

PRESS YOUR WINE:
Drain the freely running wine from the tank and put the remaining skins into a wine press. Pressing the skins gives winemakers about 15% more wine!

AGING:
Wines age in a variety of storage vessels including wooden barrels, concrete, glass, clay, and stainless steel tanks. Each vessel affects wine differently as it ages. Of course, the biggest affect is time.

BOTTLING:
It's time to bottle your wine. It's very important to do this step with as little exposure to oxygen as possible. A small amount of sulfur dioxide is often added to help preserve the wine.

ENJOY!

From Grape to Glass

White wines are the cool cats of the wine world! Unlike their bold, red counterparts, they go through a fab winemaking makeover.

After the grape harvest, white wine grapes make a quick exit from their colorful skins during the pressing phase.

By dodging prolonged skin contact, where all the color magic happens, white wines keep it fresh and fabulous. The result? A dazzling lineup of whites – from zesty and refreshing to glamorously rich and complex.

It's like a runway show of grape characteristics, strutting their stuff under the spotlight of winemaking flair and terroir vibes.

Sip, savor, and let the white wine dance party begin!

Stain the Grapes

Crafting red wine is like a passionate love story between grapes and their skins!

After the grape harvest, the magic begins. The grapes, skins and all, cozy up in fermentation, letting the skins impart color and those gorgeous tannins.

It's like the grape skins saying, "We've got this, red wine, let's make it bold and beautiful!" The result?

A sip-worthy symphony of flavor, complexity, and that unmistakable red hue.

Cheers to the art of turning grapes into a crimson masterpiece!

Sweet as a Peach

What you'll need:

- 1 bottle (750 ml) of white wine
- ½ cup (120 ml) peach schnapps
- 2 cups (480 ml) peach nectar
- ¼ cup (60 ml) fresh lemon juice
- ¼ cup (50 grams) granulated sugar
- 2 ripe peaches, sliced
- 1 cup (150 grams) fresh raspberries or strawberries
- 1 lemon, sliced
- 1-2 cups (240-480 ml) sparkling water, chilled
- Ice cubes
- Fresh mint leaves, for garnish

Method:

Step 1: Wash and slice the peaches and lemon. Wash the raspberries or strawberries.

Step 2: In a large pitcher, combine the white wine, peach schnapps, peach nectar, fresh lemon juice, and granulated sugar. Stir until the sugar is dissolved.

Step 3: Add the sliced peaches, lemon slices, and raspberries or strawberries to the pitcher. Stir gently to combine.

Step 4: Cover the pitcher with plastic wrap or a lid and refrigerate for at least 2 hours, or preferably overnight. This allows the flavors to meld together, and the fruits to infuse the sangria.

Step 5: When ready to serve, fill glasses with ice cubes. Pour the chilled Peach White Sangria into each glass, making sure to include some of the fruit pieces.

Step 6: Before serving, top each glass with a splash of chilled sparkling water or club soda, to add some effervescence and lighten the drink. Stir gently to combine.

Step 7: If desired, garnish each glass with a sprig of fresh mint leaves for a pop of color and freshness.

Your Peach White Sangria is ready to be enjoyed! Sip and savor the refreshing combination of peachy sweetness, fruity flavors, and crisp white wine.

Feel free to adjust the ingredients according to your taste preferences. You can also add other fruits like oranges, nectarines, or berries to customize your sangria.

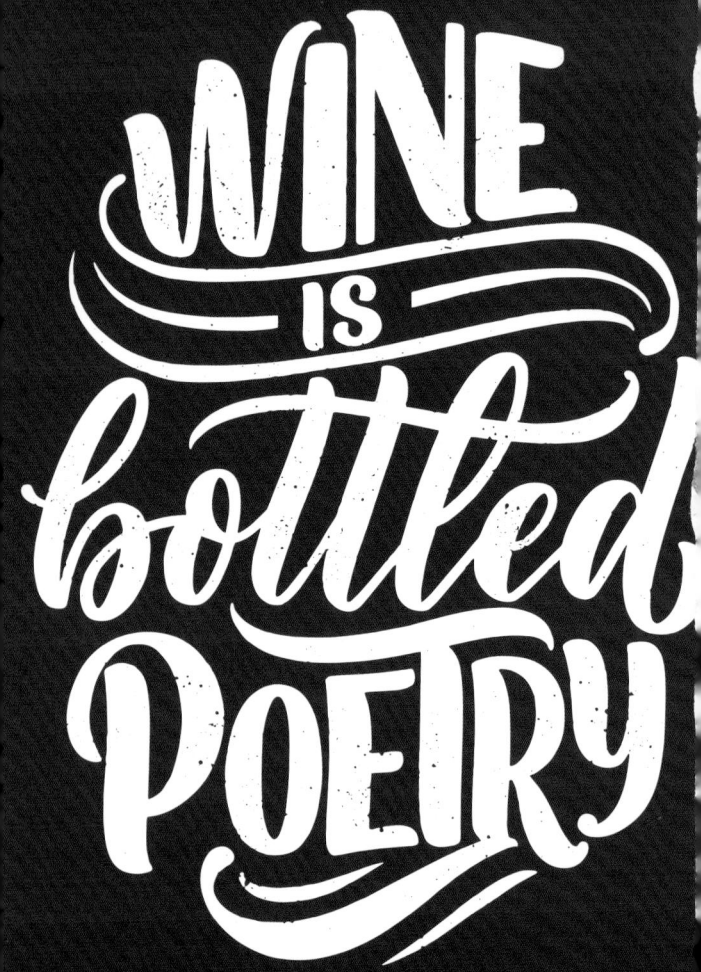